Pueblo Indian Embroidery

H. P. MERA

DRAWINGS BY THE AUTHOR

DOVER PUBLICATIONS, INC.
New York

Published in Canada by General Publishing Company, Ltd., 30 Lesmill Road, Don Mills, Toronto, Ontario.
Published in the United Kingdom by Constable and Company, Ltd., 3 The Lanchesters, 162–164 Fulham Palace Road, London W6 9ER.

Bibliographical Note

This Dover edition, first published in 1995, is an unabridged republication of the work originally published in 1943 by the Laboratory of Anthropology, Santa Fé, New Mexico, as Volume IV of their Memoirs. Three photographs were originally in color.

Library of Congress Cataloging-in-Publication Data

Mera, H. P. (Harry Percival), 1875–1951.
    Pueblo Indian embroidery / H. P. Mera.
        p.   cm.
    Originally published: Santa Fé, N. M. : University of New Mexico Press, 1943, in series: Memoirs of the Laboratory of Anthropology ; v. 4.
    Includes bibliographical references.
    ISBN 0–486–28418–2
    1. Pueblo embroidery. I. Title.
E99.P9M39   1995
746.44—dc20   94–34722
                                                                                      CIP

Manufactured in the United States of America
Dover Publications, Inc., 31 East 2nd Street, Mineola, N.Y. 11501

CONTENTS

ILLUSTRATIONS

FIGURE

PLATES

Acknowledgment

In assembling the material on which this study was based, it became necessary, due to the scarcity and wide distribution of embroidered articles, to rely on the interest and generosity of a considerable number of institutions and individuals. The response to the request for permission to use material was in every instance both prompt and unrestricted.

To Mr. F. H. Douglas the writer is particularly indebted for his kind offices in hunting out items of interest pertinent to the subject as well as for sharing information which he had been accumulating along similar lines.

Mr. K. M. Chapman was of invaluable assistance in a critical reading of the manuscript and Mrs. Kate Peck Kent furnished valuable information on prehistoric specimens which would have otherwise remained unavailable at the time of writing. Miss Helen Allen of the University of Wisconsin aided very materially by a loan of numerous publications on the subject of Old World embroidery.

Sincere thanks are also due to the following for the use of material in their possession: Field Museum of Natural History, Chicago, Ill.; Peabody Museum of Harvard University, Cambridge, Mass.; Denver Art Museum, Denver, Colo.; American Museum of Natural History, New York, N. Y.; Museum of the University of California, Berkeley, Calif.; Santa Barbara Museum, Santa Barbara, Calif.; Cranbrook Institute of Science, Bloomfield Hills, Mich.; Museum of the American Indian, Heye Foundation, New York, N. Y.; The William Rockhill Nelson Galleries of Art, Kansas City, Mo.; The Southwest Museum, Los Angeles, Calif.; Museum of Northern Arizona, Flagstaff, Ariz.; Indian Arts Fund, Santa Fe, N. M.; The Taylor Museum, Colorado Springs, Colo.; Arthur Seligman collection, Santa Fe, N. M.; Aztec Ruins National Monument, Aztec, N. M.; Fred Harvey Company, Albuquerque, N. M.; Mr. B. M. Thomas, Santa Fe, N. M.; Mr. Julius Gans, Santa Fe, N. M.; Mrs. Alta Applegate, Santa Fe, N. M.; Mr. George A. H. Fraser, Denver, Colo.; Mr. N. B. Stern, Santa Fe, N. M.; Mr. W. D. Hollister, Denver, Colo.; Mr. Theodore Van Soelen, Tesuque, N. M.; Dolores Garcia, Acomita, N. M.; and Mr. F. K. Hinchman, Los Angeles, Calif.

To these should be added those members of the Laboratory of Anthropology staff who assisted in making the publication possible, specifically Mrs. Mary M. V. Chapman who attended to typing the manuscript and business details and Mr. Stanley Stubbs for photographic work.

Finally, the author wishes to make grateful acknowledgment to the American Council of Learned Societies for the funds provided, by which a presentation of this thesis in published form has been made possible.

H. P. M.

Pueblo Indian Embroidery

HISTORY

A very distinctive type of embroidery, long produced by the Pueblo Indians of New Mexico and Arizona, is one of the least known of the several crafts practiced by these village-dwelling peoples of the Southwest. This is certainly not because of any lack of esthetic appeal nor because of an inferior technical handling, as these textiles compare very favorably in all respects with the folk-art in needle-work of European and other better known sorts. In fact, the designs employed possess a character so definitely their own that there is no possibility of confusing them with anything produced in the Old World. In addition there is a curious variation in technique which appears to be unique. Altogether it may be truthfully said that, with the exception of a scant number of European elements of late introduction, these embroideries can be considered an exemplification of a truly aboriginal American art.

One reason for the lack of a more general recognition appears to be due to the rarity of examples on which this type of embellishment appears. As a consequence of this scarcity, those who have some acquaintance with the art have long hesitated to attempt any research connected with a subject for which so little evidence now exists. The paucity of material, particularly those pieces for which dates are known, makes any attempt to trace an exact origin or a continuity of developmental stages a well-nigh impossible task. In spite of the many drawbacks to be encountered, the writer has felt that it is well worth while to gather together the information available at this time and present it in the form of a monograph in order that another Southwestern native American craft may take its place beside those of pottery-making, weaving and metal work.

After an intensive search, less than a hundred examples have been located which can be considered as representing the type of work produced previous to the 1880's. To these may be added a few owned privately and thus not listed. From fleeting glimpses and hearsay, it is believed that perhaps a dozen others may still remain in some of the Pueblos. Of those available for study, the greatest number are to be found in various museums throughout the country, the remaining being in private hands.

The reason for making a distinction between the embroideries produced before the above date and those executed in the years after that time is that obvious differences exist between what may be called the earlier or "classical" period of this art, which ended about 1880, and the somewhat inferior work of a later date.

It will no doubt be recalled that it was in the earlier years of the 1880's that the railroads began pushing into Pueblo territory. With them cheap showy prints and other machine-made fabrics put in an appearance in increasing quantities. These appear to have rapidly supplanted much of the more laboriously produced traditional handiwork. Indian villages lying nearest to the new arteries of trade were naturally the first to lose their textile crafts while others at greater distances, notably the Hopi, though considerably affected, have continued to carry on to a limited extent.

Following the close of the "classical" period, which may be said to have ended with the full establishment of rail transportation, the art of embroidery became a thing of the past in all but a very few pueblos and here it was relegated to use on fabrics principally intended for ceremonial use.

Later, in the early part of the 1920's a short-lived revival took place due to the establishment of an annual "Indian Fair" in Santa Fe, New Mexico. The sponsoring organization hoped through this means to re-establish and encourage the rapidly lapsing native arts and crafts by the awarding of prizes for meritorious work, and affording a better market.

Though some of the handicrafts in the long run were greatly benefited, work in embroidery was decidedly not one of these, and examples of needle-work which are representative of the period of this attempt at a revival are even scarcer than those of the earlier times. "Revival" embroideries, particularly those on woolen fabrics, may be readily distinguished from the classic type usually by marked differences in the character of design but more especially in the materials employed. Further mention of this matter will be made in greater detail later on.

POSSIBILITIES OF ORIGIN

Regarding the origin of Pueblo embroidery, there have been two diametrically opposing views, neither of which is backed by enough tangible evidence to constitute definite proof. Some appear to be convinced that a form of the art must have been in existence in pre-Columbian times while others have believed that it was introduced entirely from European sources. As there seems little likelihood of any very positive solution to the problem by an objective demonstration of a continuity of development, unless some unexpected evidence turns up in the future, the major arguments for both views will be briefly reviewed.

Those who support the idea of an aboriginal origin based their belief largely, until very lately, on certain passages found in the chronicles of early Spanish explorers. One of the references occurs in the account of Espejo's journey to the Pueblo country in the years 1582-83. Some of the garments seen at that time are described as having been embroidered with colored threads, others as bearing a painted decoration ("- -las mujeres traen naguas de algadon y muchas dellas borda-das con hilo de colores" and "- - y las mantas las traen puestas al uso Mexicano, aceto qui debajo de partes vergonzosas traen unos paños de algadon pintados, - -") *

Again, a year earlier than the above reference, there occurs in the *relacion* of Hernan Gallegos, chronicler of the Rodriguez expedition, mention of cotton shirts and other articles of dress, both hand-painted and embroidered. From this, it appears that a difference between the two ornamentative media was clearly recognized. On the face of all this, it has been argued that a knowledge of the technique of embroidery must necessarily have already existed at that time.

Somewhat tending to modify the force of such an argument, it may be mentioned that the word *bordado* has, at least within the last century, been used idiomatically in some of the Latin-American countries to designate textile decorative forms other than needle-work. Whether such usage obtained as early as the sixteenth century can not now be confirmed.

There is another point in connection with the visits of the early Spanish intruders that deserves consideration, but in this instance tending to favor the views of the opposition. Inasmuch as the members of the two expeditions, previously cited, were not the first whites to come in contact with these wearers of decorated cotton clothing, it might be well to see if there appears to be a possibility of a taking over of an embroidery technique during a still earlier contact with the Spanish, one which is known to have occurred during the years from 1540 to 1542.

The leader of this earlier expedition, the first of its kind into Pueblo territory, was Francisco Vasquez de Coronado. With him, besides the soldiery, were several members of a religious order and a number of Mexican Indian servants. It can be argued with some justification that certain members of this party might have been responsible to a certain degree for the decoration noted on Pueblo clothing some forty years later and which was described at that time by the term *bordado*.

The arguments for such an idea may be stated as follows: when the Coronado party finally withdrew from the country, after a period filled with misunderstandings and misfortunes, some of the clergy as well as several of the Mexican Indians were left behind. The former had doubtless come prepared to conduct missionary work and hence would have brought with them the usual vestments used in the rites of the church. Such garments were, as a rule, adorned with embroidery.

In the end, all of these missionaries were slain and their belongings, including vestments, very likely fell into the hands of the Pueblo Indians, whom they had sought to convert. The question raised is, could a people, presumed to be unfamiliar with the technique of embroidery, figure out the method from such garments and eventually apply it as an ordinary procedure to their own clothing, all within a space of forty years? It should be mentioned at this point as having some bearing

* G. P. Winship, Footnote, p. 517, part I, B.A.E. 14th An. Report.

on this matter, that it is well known to archaeologists that eyed needles were in use in prehistoric times and that sewing seams in cotton cloth and even the drawing together of worn spots by a crude form of darning has been clearly demonstrated in material from pre-Columbian times. Thus the question of an origin derived from ecclesiastical embroideries must rest wholly on a presumed ability on the part of the Indians to have successfully taken over a completely unfamiliar technical procedure from the examples obtained through the death of the missionaries, plus some knowledge of a sewing implement. If such a source be admitted, it is at least peculiar that so few traces of European embroidery techniques have succeeded in surviving.

Still another angle with relation to this same expedition remains to be discussed, this time, however, on the side of the original thesis for an aboriginal origin. The Mexican Indian servants remaining in Pueblo territory fared much better, as the accounts of the Espejo expedition of 1582-83 mention finding some of them still living in one of the Zuñi villages. But before attempting to connect these survivors with an introduction of any form of garment decoration, it will be necessary to digress for the moment.

During the last few years a considerable number of textile fragments have been unearthed by treasure seekers in various caves of the Sierra Madre mountains in the State of Chihuahua, one of the northernmost in Mexico. The materials from which these were woven include pita (agave fiber), cotton and some other vegetal fibers not yet identifiable. A large majority of these show only elemental decorative devices in the form of simple narrow stripes in dull reds and blue, while a lesser number, in striking contrast, bear elaborately conceived designs (Plates I and II). Thus far, three different techniques are recognized as having been employed: "laid in" weaving, brocading* and what appears to be a simple form of embroidery. Evidences of association with European contacts are exceedingly scant in such sites and, as far as ascertainable, these are confined to an occasional glass bead of Venetian manufacture. All designs, however, are purely aboriginal in every detail, without the slightest hint of any foreign influence.

On the basis of the scarcity of European objects, coupled with some other pertinent evidence, these textiles seem to be representative of various stages of development occurring over a considerable time interval. One such fragment was found associated with a type of pottery that apparently dates it as a product of a time as early as the thirteenth century.

If it be granted on such tenuous grounds that decorated textiles of this sort were being produced in Mexico, even as late as the arrival of Cortez in 1519, it is not beyond the bounds of possibility that one of the Mexican Indian servants left behind by the Coronado expedition might have been acquainted with some of the tex-

---

* A technique of weaving which, at times, superficially resembles embroidery.

tile decorative arts of his homeland and thus become responsible for their introduction to the Pueblos during a forty years stay among them.

Thus it is seen that there are two widely differing but possible derivations for the decorations appearing on Pueblo garments of the sixteenth century, which were termed *bordado* in the annals of that time. Neither hypothesis, however, yields satisfactory proof that one or the other is the direct progenitor of those forms which are available for study today.

Because, unfortunately, not a single authenticated example has come down to us from the early part of the historic period, it has been impossible to learn anything definite concerning the exact nature or appearance of those decorated garments which received such scant attention at the hands of the early chroniclers. Nevertheless, any article which might have survived from the earlier part of this period, even if not documented, should be easily recognized as nothing but cotton or some other vegetal fiber would have been employed for both weaving and needle-work, whereas wool embroidery appears on all known existing specimens thus marking them as produced after the arrival of sheep. These animals, it appears, were not introduced in any considerable number until sometime in the seventeenth century.

Having now discussed the two possibilities of an introduction through the agency of the Coronado expedition, attention will be called to any evidence seeming to bear on the likelihood of an origin from some other aboriginal source. Recent finds tend to offer considerable encouragement for such a view. One of these consists of a fragment of well-preserved cotton cloth bearing a design executed in an undoubted embroidery technique (Plate III). This was found in the ruins of a cliff-dwelling in Walnut Cañon near Flagstaff, Arizona. The house in which it was purportedly found has been assigned by Dr. H. S. Colton* of the Museum of Northern Arizona to the Elden Focus, an archaeological era which has been dated by dendrochronological methods as occurring during circa the twelfth century.† In the complex of traits which distinguish this focus are quite a number that denote a strong influence coming in from an area to the south.

In addition to this, three more fragmentary examples of embroidery have been lately brought to light from a locality over a hundred miles farther to the south. These were discovered by Kate Peck Kent while making a study of textile remains secured from a ruin in the Tonto National Monument, Arizona. Evidence from tree-ring data and previously determined dating for the type of pottery occurring at this site indicate an occupation in the fourteenth century. This is some two hundred years later than the date assigned to the Walnut Cañon specimen. Despite such a lapse of time, there are no evident signs of any technical advancement shown in these later examples.

* H. S. Colton, Personal communication.
† Kate Peck Kent, The Plateau, Museum of Northern Arizona, Vol. 14, No. 1, 1941, Flagstaff.

As has been previously pointed out, the art of embroidery was known, in what appears to be prehistoric times, in northern Mexico and because the use of painted or stained designs on pre-Columbian textiles is believed to have been the almost exclusive practice in the territory north of the Mogollon Rim, which is now generally conceded to be more particularly connected with purely Pueblo development, it may be reasonable to postulate a gradual northward extension of needle-work from more southerly regions.

A footnote in Amsden's Navajo Weaving*, page 117, contains the assertion that embroidery was practiced by the prehistoric peoples of the Southwest and cites specimens in the P. G. Gates collection in the Southwest Museum at Los Angeles in support of his contention. As much of this material was said to have been obtained from archaeological sites in the upper drainages of the Gila River system, or south of normal Pueblo range, an occurrence of embroidery at a point still further south than the isolated find at Walnut Cañon seems to be indicated.

These sporadic occurrences of primitive embroidery in a country where painted textile decoration was a preëminent trait prove, of course, but one thing; that decoration by means of needle-work had already become established somewhere in the Southwest as early as the twelfth century. Its rarity in the Pueblo region, as previously restricted, suggests that it may have to be viewed as an intrusion, although it must be admitted that archaeological investigation in sites favorable for the preservation of textiles has been anything but exhaustive. Outside this particular area, but still near enough to account for the transmission of a direct influence, there is the previously cited record of the thirteenth century find in northern Mexico to be kept in mind.

Taking into consideration the widely separated localities where finds have been made, it seems logical to believe that these cannot represent merely isolated instances of experiment, but would more likely postulate an intrusion from an established focus in an area not yet clearly definable. At any rate, it is difficult to credit the idea that a successful method of decoration, once attained, would be completely and permanently dropped until reintroduced through the agency of the Coronado expedition in the sixteenth century.

On the whole, it appears reasonable to tentatively accept an aboriginal origin for some form of embroidery somewhere in the Southwest, at least as early as the twelfth century, and a strong possibility of a gradual taking over and continuation of the art by Puebloan peoples from that time until the present.

Although it would have been most interesting and instructive to have been able to trace the various developmental steps from more exact sources up to the type of Pueblo embroidery as it is known today, yet it is of equal interest to realize that whatever the remote activating agencies were or the techniques involved, in time a

* C. A. Amsden, Navajo Weaving, Santa Ana, 1934. [1949 edition reprinted by Dover, 1991; ISBN 0-486-26537-4.]

school or system of decorative art has resulted which possesses a character distinct from that of any other. There is a wide difference in treatment and design from anything truly European and, at the same time, it appears not quite like that of Mexican work. On the other hand, leaving out the question of technique, there is good evidence to indicate that present-day patterns show a certain continuity of design with some of those from late prehistoric Pueblo sources, of which more later.

The "painting" of patterns on Pueblo textiles, mentioned in connection with the first documented reference to embroidery, and also noted as occurring on those of prehistoric age, was not completely supplanted by needle-work because this method of decorating is mentioned as still being in use as late as 1639, after which no further references have been found. It appears to have eventually largely died out, except for an occasional use on ceremonial dance kilts where certain symbols appear in that medium. The survival of a remnant of this method of decoration at this late date is no more than could be expected, as the application of pigments to fabrics first begins far back in Pueblo pre-history, to a time so remote that elemental finger-weaving had not yet been replaced by fabrics woven on a true loom.

GENERAL REMARKS ON DESIGN

Turning now to that portion of the subject which deals particularly with those specimens which have succeeded in surviving the wear and tear of time, an effort will be made to show the various applications of the art with an especial emphasis on design.

As a preliminary, all of these may conveniently be separated into two main categories on the basis of the materials employed in weaving. One class will include garments woven of cotton but embroidered in wool, the other includes all of those in which wool was used for both weaving and needle-work. Such a division holds true, not alone because of the types of material used, but it also carries the implication of a difference in decorative styles, although these are in no way great enough, with one exception, to indicate anything but variations of a common concept.

Generally speaking, it can be said that the designs on woolen garments have a much greater degree of complexity than do those of cotton, a number of design-units seen in the former seldom appearing on examples of the latter class. A comparative simplicity and a more marked formality are characteristic for cotton fabrics. It is not improbable that most of the present forms appearing on cotton garments may represent a type of decoration (while perhaps a little more elaborate) that is not so far removed from those first seen by the Spanish. The more complex designs appearing on woolen clothing are to be viewed as somewhat later innovations, which were developed principally in the villages of Zuñi, Acoma, and Laguna.

No differences in the basic technique of embroidery exist between the cotton and wool groups of textiles which again point to a common ancestry. The technical details of the process have been very minutely worked out by F. H. Douglas*, but for those to whom this publication is not available the method will be briefly described. The stitch used is a modification of one employed in darning, sometimes called the back-stitch. The material was comprised of two separate elements lightly twisted together, the only exception to this rule occurring during the short-lived period of a revival in the 1920's when a single strand of a four-ply commercial yarn was substituted.

The employment of an embroidery thread composed of paired and twisted elements appears to hold the answer for the successful manner in which comparatively large spaces were solidly filled in. This fashion for large solid areas, which is a characteristic, was doubtless responsible in turn for this type of sewing element and an accompanying detail which serve to differentiate Pueblo work from all other described forms of the back-stitch.

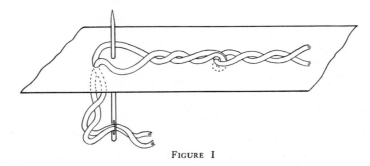

FIGURE I

In explanation, it must first be realized that in attempting to use a single stitch spanning several inches there would naturally be a sagging away from the fabric to which it was applied. Such a stitch would run the risk of being caught on any chance projection and thus be pulled loose or torn out, to say nothing of the ragged and uneven surface resulting from such a procedure.

To avoid anything of that nature an ingenious modification of the ordinary back-stitch was resorted to. Instead of a single stitch several inches long, the required length was planned to be divided into several sections in such a manner that when properly executed there is to the eye no break or offset visible. This was accomplished, after determining the desired length, by first passing the threaded needle down through the upper surface of the fabric. Then, on the reverse side, it was taken back a short distance (but only enough to firmly hold in the fabric) behind the initial point of entrance and finally returned up between the paired elements. This process could be repeated as many times as necessary to form an end to end series of stitches having the appearance of but a single continuous stitch, which also would cling closely to the underlying fabric.

* Frederic H. Douglas, An embroidered cotton garment from Acoma, Material Culture Notes. No. 1, Denver Art Museum, 1937, Denver.

After consulting numerous works on Old World embroideries, no counterpart of the two-ply method could be found nor did any of the cave fragments from Mexico show a like treatment. Because there appears to be no known source from which such a technique could have been borrowed, a local invention must be considered as probable. There is little hope of determining at just what point in the history of Pueblo embroidery it was found necessary to resort to a double yarn, but it appears that there was little need for such a procedure until fashions came into vogue wherein large spaces were required to be filled in.

If one may judge by the high development of one of the more pronounced characteristics of Pueblo embroidery design as it appears today, a unique negative treatment, a prominent feature in the present structure of design, must have begun to develop in some one of the earlier phases of the art. The term negative design is here used to describe a treatment of decorated areas wherein certain open spaces, between the masses of whatever medium is applied to a surface, are so planned as to form patterns in themselves and which thus become of principal interest. Although little direct evidence exists as to the various stages involved in the development of the Pueblo negative style, it is logical perhaps to think of its beginning as purely fortuitous.

Following the discovery that open spaces in a design could be successfully made to function as an added elaboration, there began a progressively greater development of the idea. It is also not at all improbable that such a progression might have closely followed a trend toward designs demanding the use of large solid masses of embroidery, which would seem to have required some such treatment to counteract a displeasing sense of heaviness.

That an unbroken expanse of dark color is displeasing and uninteresting seemed to have been recognized as far back as the time when the Awatovi murals (more of which later) were painted, sometime previous to the closing years of the fifteenth century. The upper part of the kilt shown in the center of Plate IV illustrates the solving of such a problem by the use of an interrupted form of negative meander. Just what relationship, if any, this figure has to the uninterrupted meanders commonly occurring on the decorative bands of cotton mantas (Plates VI and VII) cannot be directly traced, but a general similarity is quite obvious.

With results paralleling those of a search of the literature for similarities in Old World technical methods, nothing was discovered which could be considered as in any way even remotely antecedent to Puebloan styles of negative design. It is true that during the Renaissance in Europe, during the fifteenth and sixteenth centuries, some of the countries bordering on the Mediterranean produced embroideries which exhibit a certain amount of the negative pattern idea, but none has been found in which this type of decoration is so highly specialized nor forms such an important part of design.

Aside from the question of negative treatment, and perhaps the technique of application, there is obviously a greater likeness in many features of design between the type which forms the subject of this paper and that found on earlier textile decorations from northern Mexico, than there is with any of the described European styles.

As an illustration, note the general similarity of elements and organization of designs shown on Plate II and that illustrated by the drawing in the lower right hand corner of Plate X. The first represents a fragment of brocaded weaving from a cave in northern Mexico, the other is one end of an early historic embroidered breech-cloth from the Pueblo of Acoma. Both demonstrate the use of the negative pattern idea, though the latter presents it in a more highly developed form.

Another interesting comparison can be made between historic embroidery design and some decorations of prehistoric age. The latter occur on kilts depicted as worn by a number of human figures painted on the walls of a ceremonial room at the previously mentioned ruined village of Awatovi in the Hopi country (Plate IV). This chamber was unearthed beneath the remains of the old Spanish mission church at that site during investigations conducted by Dr. J. O. Brew, heading an expedition for the Peabody Museum of Harvard University. The mission at this place is documented as having been founded in 1629, so that there seems to be no question but that the room containing the murals had been in use for some time prior to that date. More positive evidence of age comes from dated beams taken from this room which have yielded, by means of dendrochronology, dates indicating occupation in the 1400's.

Compare these kilt patterns with those taken from the series of nineteenth century cotton mantas (Plates VI and VII), and a definite relationship in the structure of design can be easily recognized. These structural agreements include such basic features as a divison of the band of decoration into horizontal zones, the carrying of a color across all these divisions, thus creating a vertical sectioning of the band as well, and finally the use of a fully developed negative line treatment.

Whether the decoration appearing on the garments of these painted figures was designed to represent an application of pigment to textiles or whether needlework was intended to be represented is of course undeterminable. Dismissing the question of media, the matter of greatest moment after all lies in the obvious relationship of these designs with those of the historic period.

An examination of the types of adornment on textiles from Pueblo territory, with datings previous to the fifteenth century, disclosed but a single instance of anything that could be remotely deemed as ancestral to motifs utilized in the Awatovi mural designs, but it is also one which survives in a modified form to this day. The one occurrence is a design-unit not uncommonly used on several kinds of black-on-white pottery of the ninth century,* and which had been used in an elaborated form as a running border at the bottom of one of the Awatovi kilts which is shown in the center of Plate IV. Elemental forms of the same unit are to be seen in the drawing of the fragment of twelfth century textile shown on Plate III. It will be noticed that the principal difference lies merely in the three terminal elements which have been added to the angled hooks surmounting the row of triangles in the latter forms. In the historic version of this device these tripled elements have become fused into a single solid rectangle as in the series of hook-like elements bordering the topmost band on Plate VI.

Other sources for possible relationships in design were also sought in Pueblo basketry and pottery of pre-Columbian years but in only one instance was anything tangible discovered. This was a bowl which depicts a dancing figure clad in a kilt having a design very similar to the upper portion of the central one of the Awatovi kilts. An illustration of this bowl may be found on Plate 39, figure 1 of the Field Museum publication previously annotated. Unfortunately the type of pottery on which the dancer appears cannot pre-date the Awatovi murals by any considerable interval of time and might have even been contemporaneous.

The almost complete absence of direct prototypes in the field of decoration coming within the Pueblo area proper makes it difficult to escape the feeling that the greater share, if not all, of the more highly specialized textile designs (certainly those of the late prehistoric, early historic and later developments) will be found to stem from a source somewhere to the south, perhaps even from a locality lying as far as below the Mexican border.

It is indeed unfortunate that none of the decorated fabrics of the seventeenth and eighteenth centuries have survived, so that the course of evolution of both design and technique could have been more exactly followed. Notwithstanding this lack, a careful study of the designs here presented should make it plain to the most skeptical that they are dealing with little influenced native art forms and should some prefer to believe that the technique of embroidery was derived from a European source, then they must, at the same time admit that little more than the rudiments of a method were taken over.

It also should not be difficult to convince most any one who cares to investigate that Pueblo embroidery must be considered as having been in the past one of the outstanding outlets for artistic expression utilized by the Pueblo Indians of the Southwest.

Can such a unique and maturely developed treatment be considered as an instance of the acceptance of an idea derived from a loot of priestly vestments, even admitting some technical alterations to meet the needs of the Indian designer? It does not seem at all likely.

* Paul S. Martin and Elizabeth S. Willis, Anasazi Painted Pottery in Field Museum of Natural History, Anthropology, Memoirs of Field Museum of Natural History, Vol. 5, plate 8, Figs. 1 and 9. Chicago, 1940.

EMBROIDERIES ON COTTON

Cotton clothing worn by the Pueblo Indians of the nineteenth century, upon which wool embroidery appears, includes such articles of wearing apparel as breech-cloths, shirts, kilts, and mantas. The Spanish name for the last of these has been retained as a convenient term because this garment could be used interchangeably, either as a dress or draped over the shoulders after the manner of a shawl, no alteration of shape being required to fit it for use as one or the other. Today, the cotton manta is exclusively identified with the observance of certain ceremonial rites. Inferentially, the survival and retention of so definite a type of garment for ceremonial purposes argues for a traditional usage over what will probably prove to be a very considerable period, possibly as early as a time when loom weaving became fully established.

In addition to these items strictly intended for dress there are records that indicate the occasional use of embroidered patterns on banners which, attached to long poles, form part of the paraphernalia connected with certain dances. Customarily the decorations on these are executed in a brocade technique of weaving.

Other articles of dress which undoubtedly have as ancient a lineage as the manta are the breech-cloth and kilt. Human figures wearing the latter are shown on some of the Awatovi murals, previously mentioned in connection with the subject of design. The ornamented shirts seen by the Rodriguez expedition, on the other hand, may possibly be a somewhat later idea because, it will be remembered, there had been an opportunity to copy something of white man's clothing some forty years earlier. If an alien origin be true, any differences in structural detail between the European article and the Indian form can doubtless be laid to limitations imposed by a primitive loom.

The use of cotton for the weaving of cloth is generally accepted as extending back to at least the ninth century of the present era. Amsden* in his book on Navajo weaving has gone so thoroughly into the subject of this fiber, with its relation to southwestern weaving, that it would only be repetitious to again present the matter here.

A majority of the Navajo and all of the Pueblo weavers, as far as known, employed hand spinning for both warp and weft elements until well after the appearance of commercial cotton twine in the Southwest. After that time the latter material was sparingly utilized for warp in a limited number of Navajo blankets, the earliest of these that can be authentically dated having been woven early in the 1860's. All known Navajoan examples of this period, wherein cotton was employed for a warp, show the use of a three-ply article. At a somewhat later date four-ply cords came into use.

* C. A. Amsden, Navajo Weaving, Santa Ana, 1934. [See note on page 6.]

The Pueblo weaver, on the contrary, due to an inborn conservatism, in deference to tradition and because cotton garments were largely connected with ceremonial observances originating in the distant past, continued to spin by hand. Both warp and weft yarns were produced in this manner for a long time following the appearance of commercial twines in Navajo weaving. In the long run, however, though probably not much before 1890, the saving in labor overcame inhibitions imposed by tradition and four-ply cotton string became largely employed for the warp. Although an exception was made in the case of warp, the weft has always remained of handspun in all native loomed fabrics.

Having broken away from handwork to this extent, one might expect to find further concessions to modernization such as the adoption of machine-woven cloth for embroidering. Curious as it may seem, comparatively little commercially woven material is known to have been used for the purpose until recently, more particularly while a revival of the craft was being undertaken by certain schools conducted by the Indian Service.

Before the advent of the white man, cotton was doubtless the principal material used in embroidering and probably continued to be employed for a considerable time after the introduction of sheep or until a time when wool was being produced in quantities sufficient to supply all needs.

Not only was a change in material eventually effected but certain features of design itself probably became altered because of the use of a new medium for needle-work and perhaps equally by conditions under which the craftsman labored.

Virtual enslavement of the Indians by their conquerors doubtless greatly disturbed the old, less hurried way of life. Harassed by a constant feeling of insecurity and uncertainty, opportunities for leisurely work would have been greatly lessened so that it may well be that an effort for general effect might have taken the place of a striving for elegance of detail. Although such conditions appear to have left their permanent mark on the art as a whole, a few examples believed to have been made during the last part of the eighteenth or perhaps about the opening of the nineteenth centuries demonstrate that at least some individuals were capable of producing work with a wealth of detail. A period temporarily less turbulent and an assured economic stability may account for such as these.

At least by the beginning of the nineteenth century and from that time on, the Pueblo embroiderer employed, as far as is known, only woolen yarns for the purpose of adorning cotton textiles. In the beginning these yarns, with but few minor exceptions, were spun by hand. Later on, wherever a slight touch of contrasting color was desired, material other than that of native manufacture was occasionally substituted. Such substitutions were confined only to small areas where red was desired for purposes of accent. The reason for this innovation was probably that indigenous red dye stuffs were capable of yielding only dull rusty shades of that color, which of course suffered in comparison with the brighter hues of commercial colors.

Two types of material besides hand-spun were in use, though solely for purposes of accentuation, nearly to the three-quarter mark of the century. Both of these were commercially made products; one was a three-ply imported European article, often termed Saxony; the other being obtained by utilizing the ravelings of a trade cloth woven in England and known to the Spanish as bayeta, or, to use the English equivalent, baize. At a much later period domestic machine-made four-ply yarns were employed for the same purposes.

Fortunately these commercial yarns furnish at least some idea, which would have been otherwise lacking, as to an approximate age for the garment upon which they appear. This information came about as the result of a study of Navajo blanketry, during which it was found that imported yarns had been used in blankets which could be authentically dated all the way from the 1850's up into the middle 1870's, but not much later. After that time, four-ply kinds of American manufacture, then first coming into full production, took their places. Because Pueblo workers occasionally incorporated small amounts of such materials in their work during these same periods, a clue to age is afforded by means of the type of commercial yarn employed.

A great majority of what appear to belong to the older class of embroidered articles make use of but two principal colors, black and a dull greenish yellow shade, the latter probably having originally been of a more decided tone. An indigo blue instead of the black occurs more rarely. Also to some garments of this class were added small areas of the red just discussed. In all cases where black and yellow were used the former is greatly in the preponderance, the latter always being of secondary importance.

Most rarely seen of all, are those embroideries in which a red dyed hand-spun takes the place of black or blue as the principal color. This particular shade of red is not to be confused with the brownish tones obtained from indigenous vegetal dyes but closely resembles some of the more rose colored shades resulting from cochineal dye. So far no estimate as to age, in comparison with the less colorful varieties, has been possible, but it can be said that none of these seems to be of anything like recent manufacture. All of record appear to have originated in Acoma, a pueblo notable for unusual excellence of design and craftsmanship.

A few, patently late examples, obviously demonstrate the use of some of the more ordinary commercial dye stuffs. In addition to the colors previously mentioned, a pronounced green, undoubtedly commercial, and in one case, brown were used as an extra measure of elaboration.

By the early 1880's the craft had passed its peak and there are few signs of any further development or inventiveness in design to be seen after that time. A stereotyped conventionalism ensued far over and above that to be expected from even a normally conservative adherence to tradition. Many villages entirely ceased to produce embroidered work, but notwithstanding all this, the application of needle-work to certain cotton garments for ceremonial use has still been kept alive in some of the Hopi communities and to a lesser extent in Zuñi and Acoma.

In passing it may be a matter of some interest to know that among the Pueblos both weaving and embroidery have always been, so far as it can be ascertained, a prerogative of the men. At the present, however, women have taken up the craft, particularly those who have received instruction while attending school.

Although something of the mechanics of embroidering succeeded in surviving beyond the "classical" period, changes began to creep in, such as an increase in the use of cotton string warp in weaving and four-ply American yarns for the needle-work. The greatest break with tradition occurred within the last few years when certain educators in schools connected with the United States Indian Service have attempted to revive the art. Since that time commercially woven cloth and commercial yarns, used in single strands instead of the old paired method, are utilized in school work. As a consequence, the use of these materials has begun to spread further afield. Recently in several Pueblo communities a number of embroiderers, under white tutelage, have been engaged in decorating such items as table runners, drapes and articles of dress for sale to the public. Notwithstanding these changes, coupled with a steadily increasing exposure to alien influences, the larger aspects of design remain today not too greatly altered.

For sake of emphasis, it may be well to review the dominant features of Pueblo embroidery design with particular reference to those on cotton fabric. The most distinctive of these is to be seen in the consistent use of negative decorative elements. In fact one of the principal reliefs to the monotony of a broad band of almost solid color is furnished by these patterns, formed of narrow lines and small spaces which allow the white of the background to show through.

Another device is utilized to break up an appearance of oversolidity. This consists of several vertically placed bands executed in a color or colors contrasting with the body of the design, and spaced at such intervals as to break the band of decoration into several sections. Another characteristic feature is a series of equally spaced design-units of several kinds extending above, but usually attached to the band as a part of it. Finally there is the division of the entire decorative field into three horizontal zones of unequal width, the central one always being the narrowest. This separation is usually accomplished by means of narrow spaces or negative lines running the full length of the band. A few aberrant examples are known wherein a cord-like feature of needle-work has been substituted for the uppermost space.

This description will serve to point out the salient features of embroidery design as it occurs on Pueblo cotton textiles as a whole, but besides these basic treatments certain exceptions to the rule may occur. A clearer conception of these details can be had by consulting the illustrations and the accompanying comments.

The only units of design occurring on Pueblo embroidery that can be said to have been actually borrowed from a European source are certain highly conventionalized floral forms. A series of these units may be sometimes found barely attached to the zone beneath but in spite of this such a series is apparently counted as an uppermost zonal division itself. This observation is particularly true for woolen garments, which are to be taken up in the following section. All manifestations of this floral form are plainly modifications of, and can be traced to, a single motif. Such stylizations are believed to have been introduced by way of Mexico. Plate XIV illustrates the use of one variety of this motif on an antique Saltillo serape from that country and Plate XIII shows related forms on examples of Pueblo work.

EMBROIDERIES ON WOOL

Embroidery on woolen fabrics appears on fewer articles of dress than those woven from cotton. In fact, as far as present evidence goes, it can be said that embroidery on wool was largely limited to the adornment of the manta with records of a few decorated kilts and breech-cloths at Zuñi.

No documentary record appears to exist which specifically dates an early use of wool for the weaving of this garment but there is no doubt that so well an established form of dress was reproduced in wool, instead of cotton, once that material became available. Weaving in wool seems to have begun sometime previous to the middle of the seventeenth century when it appears that enough of that commodity was being grown to supply an amount over and above the needs of the colonists for their own use. This is plainly shown by a trade invoice of 1638 which lists the contents of a substantial shipment of textiles of various sorts, including many woolen fabrics which had been consigned to Mexico for sale.* Among the items listed are one hundred and twenty-six small blankets which probably referred to mantas, but unfortunately in this particular instance no specific mention is made of the material from which they were woven.

The earliest known example for which an approximate dating can be given is in the possession of the Laboratory of Anthropology (Plate XV). It was found under conditions and in association with other material which definitely mark it as a product of either the last part of the eighteenth or the very beginning of the nineteenth centuries. Although not embroidered, it is technically the same in all respects as others of a later date, upon which it was customary to apply such decoration.

*L. B. Bloom, A trade invoice of 1638, New Mexico Historical Review, Vol. X, No. 3, pp. 242-248, 1935, Albuquerque.

The body of this specimen was woven from dark brown hand-spun yarn, the natural color of the so-called black sheep, in a diagonal twill technique. It is bordered on both edges of its longest dimension by bands, five inches in width, done in a diamond twill or goose-eye weave. Indigo blue hand-spun was used for the latter feature. Because all recorded woolen mantas since that time are natural brown or dyed black with blue borders, with but two exceptions where a blue, so deep in tone that it is almost black, was employed, it follows that the fashion for these somber hued garments must have become fixed previous to the beginning of the nineteenth century.

Although the weaving of diagonal and diamond twills was not an uncommon practice on cotton textiles in prehistoric times, it is more rarely seen on historic pieces wherein that fiber was employed. Plate XVI illustrates a fragment of prehistoric cotton cloth showing both herringbone and diamond patterns in twilled weaving. The survival and continuation of a technique derived from an earlier period appears to offer a reasonable explanation for its later use in post-Spanish woolen garments. Some form of the diagonal twill is always used for the main portions of all observed wool mantas while the borders may be woven in either a diamond or herringbone twill. Black twilled mantas, either with or without embroidery, to this day are still in demand among the Pueblos for occasions where native costumes are a requisite, such as feasts, dances and like observances.

The foregoing description will give some idea of the garment on which appear some of the most striking embroidery designs ever produced by the Pueblo craftsman. Although the kind having woven diamond twill borders was sometimes utilized for embroidery by merely working over and hiding that feature, others were woven especially to receive needle-work. These latter substitute a plain weave for the patterned borders of the former thus making it much easier to space more accurately the various elements of design by counting the webb threads.

There is still another variation which incorporates the diamond twill border into the general scheme of decoration (Plates XXI and XXII). This is accomplished by allowing it to remain uncovered but surrounding it with needle-work, a principal band of design being embroidered just above the twilled portion with narrower edgings enclosing the remaining three sides. Where this was done, the old idea of dividing the field of decoration into three zones is maintained, if the band of twilling is counted as one of the zones.

The materials used in embroideries on wool up to the early 1880's are the same as those employed on cotton fabrics from the same time levels, hand-spun in twisted pairs by far predominating. Bayeta, a yarn composed of ravelings from an imported trade cloth, came next in importance while the three-ply imported sort, occurring in small amounts on cotton textiles, is mostly rarely met with. In fact, as far as has been determined at this time, only two examples are known which demonstrate any use at all of the last mentioned (Plate XXIII).

The reason for the greater relative importance of bayeta as a medium for embroidery on wool over its use on cotton rests in the color, a rich lake red. Whereas small quantities of this color were used in embroideries on cotton garments principally for the purposes of accenting certain minor features of design, it served as the dominant color on many of the dark wool mantas, bringing the entire pattern into striking contrast with the somber hued background.

Later, during the previously mentioned short-lived revival in the 1920's, embroideries employed nothing but four-ply commercial yarns of various sorts, all of American manufacture. These yarns have been popularly classed under the inclusive term of "Germantown," a designation derived from a town of that name in Pennsylvania where one of the first mills to manufacture four-ply domestic yarn was situated.

Machine-spun material, on the other hand, appears never to have entered into the weaving of the wool manta. In this respect its history does not parallel that of cotton fabrics wherein commercial string was used as a warp in its later phases. When recently woven woolen garments of this class are examined it will be found that nothing but hand-spun yarn is present.

In passing, it may be of interest to note that in most of the examples bearing "revival" embroideries of the 1920's, mantas had been chosen which plainly show the wear of many years use before receiving their embellishment of needle-work.

Before taking up any general features of woolen manta design, it is important to call attention to the fact that only three villages appear to have been concerned to any considerable extent in embroidering on wool, in addition to that on cotton, in the pre-1880 period. Though a number of other communities continued to practice the art on articles of clothing woven from the latter fiber, work on wool appears to have held little interest. The three are Acoma, Laguna and Zuñi.

Only the first two of these appear to have more directly derived their designs from the traditionally stylized forms common to most cotton mantas, a situation which would naturally be expected as the result of a logical development from an old established usage. Zuñi work, on the contrary, made use of a system which is, in most cases, entirely different in character from anything known to be in any way antecedent, although the full use of a form of negative treatment was preserved (Plate XXV). The Zuñians seem to have broken away from anything resembling the old fundamental style but one which they still, curiously enough, continued to use concurrently on cotton textiles. Just what prompted such a radical change, particularly in the face of the Pueblo's inborn tenacity of purpose in clinging to traditional usage, has not been made clear. The possibilities of origins for these Zuñi woolen manta designs from sources other than those found on textile decoration have been sought, but so far without success.

There is another noticeable difference besides the character of design, that sets the work of the Zuñi craftsmen apart from those of Acoma and Laguna. The embroiderers of the latter two communities favored red, blue and green, the red being of primary importance, while in Zuñi the blue was used almost exclusively, only a few exceptions to the rule having been noted. The reason for this preference for blue designs on a black background is hard to explain as that color is often so dark in tone that it is hardly distinguishable at times.

Acoma designs, as well as those of Laguna, on the whole are characterized by a wider range in the number of decorative elements and by less rigidity of style than is to be found on cotton garments. The use of the negative treatment continued to hold an important place and remained a dominant feature. Everything being taken into consideration it can be seen that altogether there tends to be a somewhat greater sense of lightness when compared to the work on the typical cotton manta.

Still following the ancient formula, a division of the band of decoration into three more or less separate horizontal zones is made although the relative widths of these features have undergone a transposition. The lowest of these has become the widest; the second, a narrow strip, comes next and above this is a series of design-units, sometimes attached, but as frequently separated from the narrow strip below, which in effect, can be said to amount to a third.

One of the distinctive features always present in cotton manta designs is entirely lacking in those of wool. These are the vertically placed stripes of contrasting color that extend through the full width of the band of embroidery and serve to divide it into sections. Although a secondary color is often used on wool mantas, it does not take the form of a vertical stripe. Each zone of the band is treated independently by interspersing various shaped masses of a subordinate color at intervals along its length. Another feature calling for comment is that the arrangement and spacing of the elements of design in any given zone are seldom planned with a particular reference to the decorative schemes occurring in any other zone in the same band of decoration. Each, in the mind of the designer, seems to have been thought of and executed as a primarily distinct entity, but at the same time it must have been also recognized as an integral component in a larger design structure.

As in the case of cotton garments, the only intrusive elements in design are furnished by various adaptations of the same floral motif previously mentioned. Among the Zuñi these were used quite simply, but in Acoman work they were more often paired in such a manner as to virtually constitute a single unit. It is most interesting to see how some workers have appeared to be conscious of the fact that this symbol, in reality represents a stylized flower, while to others nothing of the original idea seemed to have remained. This is particularly true in regard to late usage.

Another very interesting item connected with the use of these borrowed elements lies in the fact that a satin stitch is always employed when embroidering these units instead of the normal Pueblo back-stitch. This would doubtless imply that not only was an alien decorative form adopted but a new technique was taken over as well for the particular purpose.

Other forms of non-native stitches also have been used at times, such as buttonholing for binding edges and a chain-stitch when thin lines are desired, but in the main body of design only the traditional back-stitch appears.

AN EXPLANATION OF THE DRAWINGS OF DESIGN

As an aid to a better understanding of the plates upon which drawings of the various designs appear, there are a number of points to be brought out regarding the reasons for the manner in which they were executed. All of these have to do with an effort to adopt a form of presentation that would furnish some common basis for comparative purposes.

Because it was found inexpedient to use the original colors, black and white have been substituted. The dominant color is always indicated by solid black while those of secondary importance are shown by stippling and hachure. This procedure does not result in any very serious drawback as the structure of design and not the coloring is the principal concern. A color key, however, has been provided in each instance. Another advantage is gained by this method, in that all designs appear on a white background thus bringing out negative features to the fullest extent, an especially desirable state of affairs in the case of those embroideries occurring on dark materials.

Those who have some familiarity with Pueblo embroidery may, perhaps, at first wonder at the rigid stylization of the drawings as compared to the somewhat less formal effects seen on actual specimens. The decision to use this treatment came as the result of a critical appraisement of the material to be used in this paper. It was found that a very considerable range of technical ability was involved, some of the poorer examples showing a decidedly indifferent quality of work, while others displayed a high degree of craftsmanship. With this situation in mind, it was finally deemed best to formalize everything equally, as, after all, it is the intent of design rather than the inequalities of workmanship that should be illustrated. Nevertheless, no detail of design or its relative placement has been in any way altered.

Another matter demanding explanation has to do with the treatment accorded the series of floral conventionalizations surmounting many of the bands of decoration. As there is apt to be a considerable variation, sometimes very pronounced, among the several floral units occurring in any given band, some particular form representing an average for a series or one having a distinctive character has been chosen for illustration. In this way it has been possible to show the principal variations encountered by a comparison of all the drawings on which these motifs appear.

Plates

PLATE I

FRAGMENT OF TEXTILE FROM CHIHUAHUA, MEXICO

This was found in a cave in the State of Chihuahua, Mexico, where it was unearthed by treasure seekers. All warp elements are single ply and hand-spun from agave fiber, the weft threads from cotton. The design has been worked in a two-ply thread also hand-spun from cotton and dyed a light blue. Due to the condition of the specimen, it has proved puzzling to exactly determine the method employed in producing the ornamentative features. There are but two possibilities however; brocading during the process of weaving or by means of a darning stitch after the loosely woven fabric was completed.

In its present state it measures about 43x50 inches.

LABORATORY OF ANTHROPOLOGY

PLATE I

PLATE II

FRAGMENT OF TEXTILE FROM CHIHUAHUA, MEXICO

Another specimen of antique textile art from burial caves in northern Mexico. In this instance, unlike the example illustrated on Plate 1, a brocading technique was definitely used to effect the design. All weaving elements have been spun from cotton. The color scheme is blue and white, the first mentioned being of a much darker shade than that described for the example on the preceding plate.

Only the extreme dryness of the caves, in which such remnants were discovered, can account for so good a state of preservation.

LABORATORY OF ANTHROPOLOGY

PLATE II

PLATE III

FRAGMENT OF PREHISTORIC EMBROIDERY AND
A RECONSTRUCTION OF DESIGN

Cotton appears to be the only fiber utilized for both weaving and embroidery. Although too fragile to admit of much handling, the dominant features could be adequately made out. The most obvious of the embroidered portions appear to have been executed in something like a satin stitch, using a thread dyed with a color which has since faded to an indeterminate grayish cast.

Not as noticeable as the grayish colored series of angular hook-like devices are other less well preserved remains of needle-work which were traceable to areas corresponding with the stippled portions shown in the reconstruction of design. Present appearances point to some shade of yellow as the original color.

This small piece of textile was found in an association with other factors that assign to it a probable date of as early as the twelfth century.

MUSEUM OF NORTHERN ARIZONA

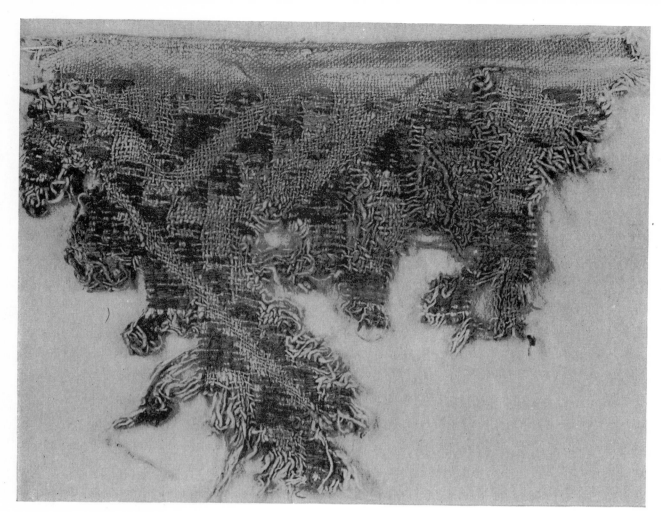

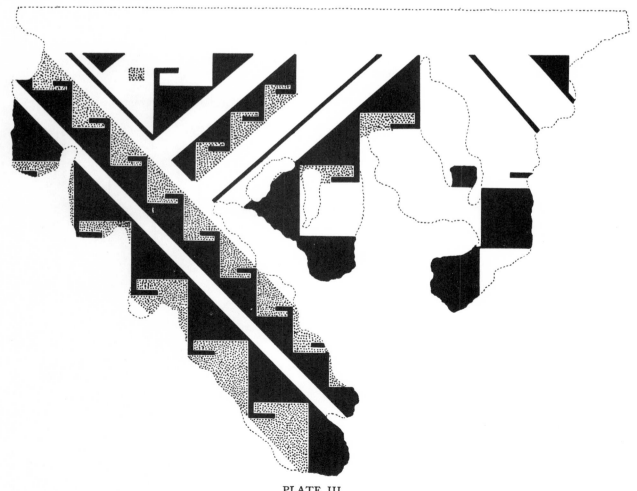

PLATE III

Plate IV

TEXTILE DESIGNS FROM THE AWATOVI MURALS

The designs figured here were taken from wall paintings in a ceremonial room in the abandoned Pueblo of Awatovi. From beams used in roofing this structure, dates were obtained indicating the room was still in use until sometime in the fifteenth century. All the drawings represent decorations used on kilt-like garments depicted as being worn by dancers or perhaps mythological personifications.

The central figure shows an entire kilt with both a decorative band at the bottom and a broken meander device in the negative above. This latter appears to bear some relationship to those negative line meanders that hold such a prominent place in historic embroidery design. The others are patterned bands on the lower part of otherwise undecorated garments of that same kind.

In the historic period, as far as is known, ornamental strips of embroidery are applied to dance kilts, not horizontally as is shown here, but vertically at both ends of a length of fabric which comprises the kilt.

Note the basic similarities in design structure between these examples of prehistoric age and those of later times shown on the following three plates. These similarities are: the use of terraced arrangements composed of triangular forms; a division of the band into several zones, usually three in number; the use of negative line patterns and a tendency to carry one of the colors across two or more of the zones.

Color key: solid areas, black; stippling, red.

PEABODY MUSEUM OF HARVARD UNIVERSITY

PLATE IV

PLATE V

AN EMBROIDERED COTTON MANTA OF THE MID-NINETEENTH CENTURY

Size: 41x50 inches.

LABORATORY OF ANTHROPOLOGY

PLATE V

PLATE VI

DESIGNS FROM AN ACOMAN COTTON MANTA

Here is shown the usual arrangement of embroidered areas on a typical cotton manta.

Where a difference in width exists between the two bands, that on the bottom is always the wider and extends the full width of the fabric. The upper, besides being normally narrower, is also shorter, leaving an undecorated space in both upper corners of the garment to allow the bringing of the two together for pinning across the wearer's chest when worn as a shawl. Leaving these corners bare appears to be purposeful as it was probably found that the heavy hand-wrought pins used for the purpose would have caused some damage to any embroidery occurring in such a position.

While there is, within certain limits, some variation seen in the lower bands of design in a majority of the examples examined, few changes from a stereotyped treatment have been observed for the upper bands. For this reason only those are figured in the following plates which possess features diverging from the typical.

The two decorative devices just beneath the upper band mark this manta as a product of the Pueblo of Acoma. Figures of this sort are said to have been used by no other village.

Attention is particularly directed to a bordering of slanted and angled hook-like motifs on the upper band which were no doubt derived from the same ancestral form as those at the bottom of the central design on Plate IV. Variations of this same device can be seen on Plates XI and XXII.

Color key: solid areas, black; stippling, red.

LABORATORY OF ANTHROPOLOGY

PLATE VI

PLATE VII

DESIGNS FROM COTTON MANTAS

On this plate are figured four variations of a generalized style which is to be found on the lower bands of a majority of all cotton garments of this class. The upper bands for these have not been figured as they do not differ materially from that shown on the preceeding plate.

Proceeding from top to bottom, the uppermost decorative band shows that the embroiderer in this case so erred in spacing the several parts of the design that when the right hand end was reached there was insufficient room for a complete section to match that on the other. Such gross error in spacing is rarely seen.

Color key: solid areas, black; stippled stripes, green; stippled figures, red.

ARTHUR SELIGMAN COLLECTION

In the one next below, prominent colored motifs have been introduced to add to the interest of a design which, in the main, follows an established formula.

Color key: solid areas, black; stippling, yellow; hatching, red.

LABORATORY OF ANTHROPOLOGY

Below this is another where a curious combination of color and open spaces have been used to provide variety.

Color key: solid areas, black; stippling, green; hatching, red.

DENVER ART MUSEUM

As compared to the others above it, the example at the bottom exhibits a much less complicated arrangement of negative line pattern and an extra color has been used in the form of some stepped figures which occupy an out of the ordinary position.

Color key: solid areas, black; stippling, green; hatching, red.

DENVER ART MUSEUM

PLATE VII

35

PLATE VIII

DESIGNS FROM COTTON MANTAS

All designs here illustrated were taken from two mantas. Upper and lower bands for each are shown as both possess features that are unique. The narrower band of the uppermost pair displays a series of points along the lower margin instead of the usual array of slanted hook-like elements. Also both upper and lower bands exhibit negative line patterns quite at variance with those most commonly seen.

Color key: solid areas, black; stippling, green; hatching, red.

DENVER ART MUSEUM

As regards the lower pair, not only are many features in the structure of design aberrant but also the principal color is unusual in mantas where design units comprised of terraced arrangements of triangular forms are a conventional treatment.

The upper band has also departed even more from the typical in that some of the negative line patterns can be traced to those usually occurring on bottom bands, and the stripes of contrasting color have been widened and are not used in pairs.

Color key: solid areas, blue; stippling, red; hatching, yellow.

AMERICAN MUSEUM OF NATURAL HISTORY

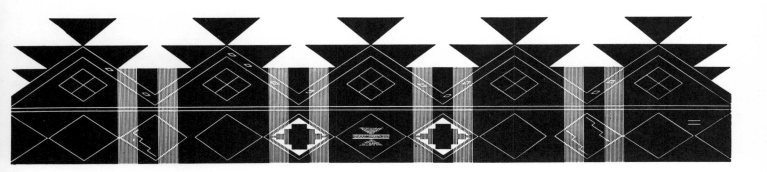

PLATE VIII

PLATE IX

DESIGNS FROM COTTON MANTAS

The two central designs were taken from the same garment. Both of these are alike in structural principles with similar examples illustrated on Plate V, though a great deal of extra elaboration has been employed. The color scheme is also uncommon. No upper band has been figured as it differs from the average only in certain minor changes made in order to match the style of the lower.

Color key: solid areas, rose; stippling, black; hatching, green.

LABORATORY OF ANTHROPOLOGY

Above these is one of the most unusual examples of embroidery discovered during the selection of material for this paper. Not only is the design at variance with ordinary usage but the embroidery stitches, instead of running vertically, as in other known specimens, were made horizontally. The series of stems with conventionalized leaves surmounting the band were undoubtedly borrowed from an alien source as also is the satin stitch with which they were worked. That this design-unit represents a plant form will become more apparent when attention is directed to the band at the bottom of the plate. Both upper and lower bands are alike in this respect, an unusual circumstance in itself on cotton mantas.

Color key: solid areas, red; stippling, blue.

DENVER ART MUSEUM

The drawing at the bottom illustrates another very interesting breaking away from the more traditional form of decoration. Although apparently based on the treatment most frequently employed for upper bands on cotton mantas, its vertical stripes of contrasting color, as has been already noted for an upper band on the previous plate, have been greatly widened and used singly instead of in the more customary pairs. Here again a series of stylized plant forms surmount the main band of design. These differ from similar decorative units at the top of the page in that there are unquestionable floral elements (Plate XIII) incorporated in the bases of each unit, which would again tend to confirm the belief that such designs may be viewed as plant adaptations. A foreign source is also postulated for this particular form because of the use of a satin stitch, all other points of the design being executed in the stitch which is distinctive of Pueblo work. In this instance also, both the upper and lower bands on the manta have been designed alike.

Color key: solid areas, rose; stippling, black; hatching, green.

FIELD MUSEUM OF NATURAL HISTORY

PLATE IX

PLATE **X**

DESIGNS FROM COTTON BREECH-CLOTHS

All but one of these examples adhere strictly to the rule that requires a division of the field into three zones and that one (upper left), perhaps as a concession to convention, shows a trace of the idea which is to be seen in the two short horizontal negative lines dividing the stripes of contrasting colors into three vertical sections.

In every instance it has been possible to trace these examples to the pueblo from which they came. The one in the upper right hand corner was obtained from the Pueblo of Jemez, the remainder from Acoma. All are badly worn, in rather poor condition and appear to be of a greater age than any other piece of embroidery thus far examined. There is quite a variety of color exhibited in the group. From left to right, beginning at the top the combination of colors for each are listed as follows:

Color keys: solid areas, blue; stippling, green; vertical hatching, brown; horizontal hatching, red.

DENVER ART MUSEUM

Solid areas, black; stippling, red.

INDIAN ARTS FUND COLLECTION

Solid areas, black; stippling, green; hatching, red.

DENVER ART MUSEUM

Solid areas, blue; stippling, green; hatching, black.

DOLORES GARCIA, OWNER

Solid areas, blue; stippling, green; hatching, brownish red.

DOLORES GARCIA, OWNER

Solid areas, blue; stippling, green; hatching, brownish red.

INDIAN ARTS FUND COLLECTION

PLATE X

41

PLATE XI

DESIGNS FROM COTTON KILTS

As noted in the remarks accompanying Plate IV, embroidered bands occurring on all known kilts of historic age are arranged vertically on the garment, whereas those pictured in wall paintings executed in prehistoric times indicate some form of decoration placed horizontally, parallel with the lower margin. There is no exact information as to when this change took place. A hint in this direction is furnished by two plates (Nos. 1 and 2) in a report of an expedition down the Zuñi and Colorado Rivers in 1851, under the command of Captain L. Sitgreaves. The plates were made from drawings by R. H. Kern of Zuñi Indians wearing kilts which were bordered by decoration around their lower margins. Whether the artist made his sketches from observation or merely from information is not clear. The same remarks hold true for an illustation of Jemez Indians, by the same artist, to be found in J. H. Simpson's account of an expedition into the Navajo country in 1852.

The four designs having the greatest length illustrate some of the styles which have been and are still in use. The two toward the right are variations of the type most commonly seen. It will be noted that both of these latter have symbols incorporated which represent clouds and rain, terraced figures standing for the former and a series of lines indicating the latter. The three smaller detached drawings are other interpretations of the cloud-rain concept found on kilts.

A division of the band of decoration into three zones is maintained in all examples examined. The basic structural features closely agree with those to be found on the upper bands of the standard cotton manta (Plate VI), although there is some latitude in the use of the characteristic transverse stripes of contrasting color. In the two left hand designs these have been greatly widened and used singly instead of in the more usual manner which calls for a paired arrangement as demonstrated in the two right hand drawings.

From left to right, the colors used in embroidering and the ownership of the garments from which the four larger designs were taken are given.

Color keys: solid areas, red; stippling, blue.

DOLORES GARCIA, OWNER

Solid areas, red; stippling, blue.

DOLORES GARCIA, OWNER

Solid areas, black; stippling, red; hatching, yellow.

INDIAN ARTS FUND COLLECTION

Solid areas, black; stippling, red; hatching, green.

INDIAN ARTS FUND COLLECTION

Ownership cannot be given in case of the three small drawings as these were obtained from sketches made from kilts worn by dancers during a ceremony.

Color key for all: solid areas, black; stippling, red; hatching, green.

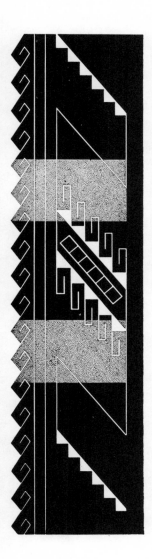
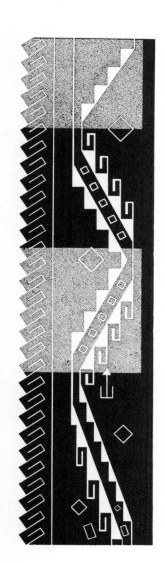

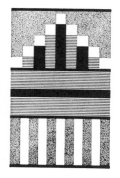

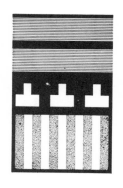

PLATE XI

PLATE XII

A PUEBLO EMBROIDERED COTTON SHIRT

Length from neck to hem, 23 inches.

DENVER ART MUSEUM

PLATE XII

PLATE XIII

DESIGNS FROM COTTON SHIRTS

Pueblo cotton shirts were frequently lavishly embellished with needle-work, not only around the bottoms but at the cuffs, over shoulder seams and about the neck. In addition to these more solid bands of embroidery, isolated cruciform units were distributed symmetrically over the body and sleeves. Usually the same motifs were consistently used in decorative bands throughout all parts of a garment, but in at least one instance a substitution was made. This is illustrated by the band of design at the bottom of the plate and the large rectangular drawing of a pattern, intended for decoration of the shoulders, immediately above it to the left, both from the same garment. In this instance all but the area over the shoulder seams conform with the arrangement of motifs in the lower figure.

In none of the five bands of shirt decoration depicted here does there appear to be any of the typically conventional division into three zones, though all may be said to carry it out in principle, provided that the row of floral stylizations and terraced figures be considered as an uppermost zone. That such a view is within the bounds of reason will be made more apparent when the designs characteristic of woolen mantas are described, to which shirt decoration will in many respects be found to be closely related.

Another matter worthy of note is that no negative line has been left open to separate the lower zone from the next above it, with one exception, the rectangular arrangement above and to the left of the bottom band. All this notwithstanding, a division is clearly recognized, both by reason of differences in type of design between the two zones but also by their having been worked separately, the terminal stitches of the lower zone meeting with the beginning stitches of the one above along a line where normally a narrow opening separating the two is left.

Paired stripes of contrasting color noticeable in manta decoration seem to have been entirely discarded in favor of single wide areas which only occasionally (second band from the bottom) traverse all three zones.

Three examples of variation in cruciform devices are shown opposite the ends of the bands with which they were in association.

The topmost figure and the accompanying cross-like symbol were taken from a shirt embroidered during a short-lived revival of the art in the 1920's. Motifs in the two lower zones of the decorative band from this same garment have been found to duplicate those on others from the old "classical" period. However in the older, floral conventionalizations took the place of the terraced figures shown here.

The following keys to color are given, beginning at the top: solid areas, red; stippling, black.

INDIAN ARTS FUND COLLECTION

Solid areas, red; stippling, blue.

DENVER ART MUSEUM

Solid areas, blue; stippling, red.

AMERICAN MUSEUM OF NATURAL HISTORY

Solid areas, red; stippling, blue.

FRED HARVEY COLLECTION

Solid areas, red; stippling, blue.

SANTA BARBARA MUSEUM OF NATURAL HISTORY

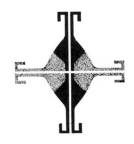
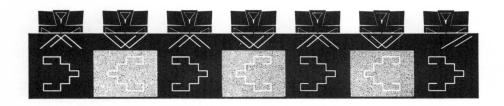

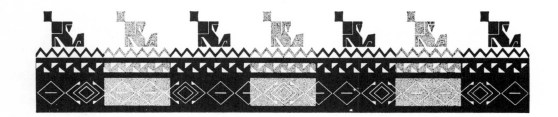

PLATE XIII

SECTION OF A SALTILLO SERAPE SHOWING FLORAL MOTIFS

A double row of floral conventionalizations may be seen in the lower portion of the illustration. Forms of this motif were among the practically negligible number of design elements to appear on Indian embroideries which can be in any way definitely traced to an alien source. Several variations can be seen on the preceding plate and on Plate XXV.

In some embroideries on wool, as will be seen, it becomes paired and when in this form, is then apparently regarded as a complete unit.

THE TAYLOR MUSEUM

PLATE XIV

Plate XV

AN ANTIQUE WOOLEN MANTA

From circumstances under which this garment was found and because of the character of the material with which it was associated, a consensus of competent opinion places it as a product of a time at least as early as the beginning of the 1800's.

Hand-spun wool, selected from black sheep, was employed for weaving, except for the borders where a blue weft element had been introduced to create a goose-eye or diamond twill pattern.

This early form of woolen manta differs in no essential detail from those which, at a later time, bore elaborate designs in needle-work.

Size: 46x63 inches.

LABORATORY OF ANTHROPOLOGY

PLATE XV

PLATE XVI

FRAGMENT OF PREHISTORIC TWILLED WEAVING IN COTTON

Examples of fabrics showing a knowledge of twilled weaving in prehistoric times are not uncommon, some even dating as far back as the twelfth century. This fragment not only exhibits a herringbone pattern in that technique but a diamond twill as well. This specimen is by no means unique as a number of other examples are known. The technical handling required to produce the diamond effect in this piece is the same as that used for the purpose of weaving the borders of the woolen manta illustrated on the preceding plate. Excavated at the Aztec Ruin, near Aztec, New Mexico, a date of not later than the middle of the thirteenth century is thought to be approximately correct for the specimen.

All this plainly proves that the diamond twill is not the result of white man's influence as many have supposed.

AZTEC RUINS NATIONAL MONUMENT MUSEUM

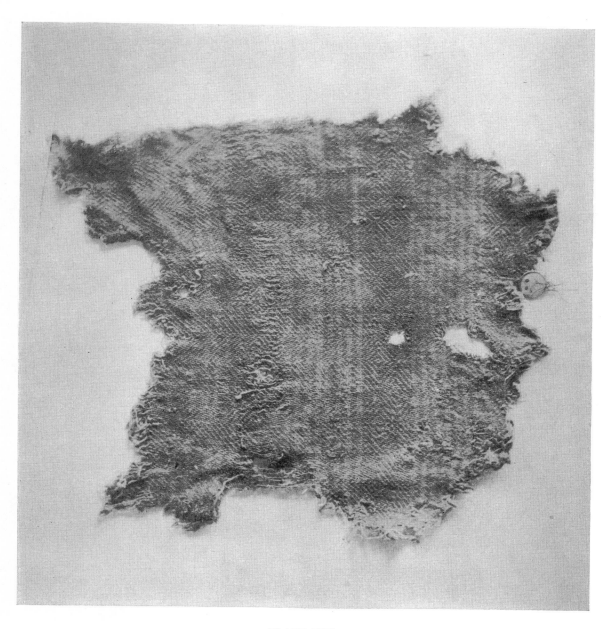

PLATE XVI

PLATE XVII

A LATE NINETEENTH CENTURY EMBROIDERED WOOLEN MANTA

This particular manta has been chosen to illustrate the type because negative patterns show to a greater advantage when the colors used in embroidering on a dark ground are comparatively light in tone. Also it has the distinction of being one of the very few recorded examples where a very dark shade of blue hand-spun yarn has been substituted for the more conventional brown or black.

Size: 39x49 inches.

LABORATORY OF ANTHROPOLOGY

PLATE XVII

PLATE XVIII

DESIGNS FROM WOOLEN MANTAS

In any discussion of embroidery on woolen fabrics, it is well to realize that garments woven from that material are by no means a late development. The woolen manta as such, with little doubt, first made an appearance soon after that fiber was introduced to the Indian weaver about three hundred years ago, though just when the embellishment of this article of clothing by needle-work was first undertaken remains an unanswerable question.

It should also be kept in mind that embroidery on both cotton and wool flourished side by side over a considerable span of years, each class, as will be seen, exhibiting distinctive ideas about decorative values. Why the generally less complicated patterns of the cotton garment were not copied on those of wool may be explained by the fact that certain decorative forms, and cotton fabrics as well, may have been considered as they are today, traditional adjuncts connected with ceremonialism, while more freedom of expression was allowable on things intended principally for personal adornment. Be this as it may, the differences between the two are not quite so fundamental as it may appear at first glance.

One of the principal basic treatments to be sought in relating the two types of design is whether a division of the band into three zones can be found in the woolen article. This must hinge largely on the question as to whether the series of detached motifs surmounting the two zones beneath them can properly be recognized as being to all intents and purposes, a third. The band of decoration, second above the bottom, appears to present some support for such a view, in that modifications of the terraced arrangements of triangles occupy a location comparable with similar figure connected with third zone treatments on cotton fabrics. If it be admitted that the series of motifs in reality constitute a third and upper zone then the proportionate widths of the two outside zones have become reversed. From the fifteenth century on through all periods of designing for use on cotton, the uppermost zone of the bottom band was, as a rule, the widest but in work on wool the bottom zone on the contrary possesses the greatest width. Despite this, it is believed that a three zone division was perpetuated, at least in principle.

Another transference of form, though not of function, is seen in a consistent change from the characteristic paired vertical stripes of a secondary color to broader areas that do not carry uninterruptedly through all zones as did the former. These areas of contrasting color are used in two ways. The simpler form consists of what may be called panels evenly spaced throughout the length of the median and lower zones, not always with any particular reference to the placement of those on the adjacent zone. This type is well illustrated in the example next below the upper band on the plate.

In the other, the areas of secondary coloring, instead of serving merely as backgrounds, have been converted into various decorative shapes that are used to add further elaboration to the general scheme of design. The lower zone of the topmost drawing and that of the second below it demonstrate such a use.

Attention is also directed to the fact that unlike cotton mantas no difference in lengh or width is made between the upper and lower decorative bands.

Color keys are given below beginning at the top: solid areas, red; stippling, blue.

FRED HARVEY COLLECTION

Solid areas, red; stippling, greenish blue.

DENVER ART MUSEUM

Solid areas, red; stippling, blue.

INDIAN ARTS FUND COLLECTION

Solid areas, red; stippling, green.

FIELD MUSEUM OF NATURAL HISTORY

PLATE XVIII

Plate XIX

DESIGNS FROM WOOLEN MANTAS

The explanatory remarks opposite the preceding plate will apply equally to this and the next in order.

The color keys are given in order from above, downward: solid areas, red; stippling, green.

UNIVERSITY OF CALIFORNIA MUSEUM

Solid areas, red; stippling, blue.

ARTHUR SELIGMAN COLLECTION

Solid areas, red; stippling, blue.

B. M. THOMAS COLLECTION

Solid areas, red; stippling, blue.

JULIUS GANS, OWNER

PLATE XIX

59

PLATE **XX**

DESIGNS FROM WOOLEN MANTAS

Note the unsymmetrical treatment of the design in the lower zone of the topmost decorative band. In fact, a close scrutiny of all of the wool manta designs will disclose a number of such discrepancies, although not so obviously inconsistent.

An interesting instance of the carrying over of a decorative device from an earlier period is seen in the vertical series of outlined lozenge-shaped units in the lowest zone of the band, second from the bottom. Compare these with similar arrangements shown in the upper zone of the example figured in the lower right-hand corner of Plate X.

Color keys from top to bottom: solid areas, red; stippling, blue.

LABORATORY OF ANTHROPOLOGY

Solid areas, red; stippling, greenish blue.

CRANBROOK INSTITUTE OF SCIENCE

Solid areas, red; stippling, blue.

LABORATORY OF ANTHROPOLOGY

Solid areas, red; stippling, blue.

INDIAN ARTS FUND COLLECTION

PLATE XX

61

PLATE **XXI**

DESIGNS FROM WOOLEN MANTAS

The designs shown on this and the following plate represent a well marked style in which a portion of the fabric is utilized in the decorative scheme. The part chosen for incorporation is that woven diamond twill or goose-eye strip which normally forms a border on many of both cotton and woolen mantas. To obtain this effect blue weft threads are introduced into the web at the proper place during the weaving process. By framing this twill-woven border with needle-work, it becomes an integral part of the decorative band.

Again a question rises as to whether such a procedure was a deliberately conceived effort to largely conform to the traditional three zone division of a decorative band, using the twilled weaving as the lowest. But after examining the drawings on this and the next plate it will be seen that all of the examples illustrated do not precisely conform to that idea, depending however on the individual interpretation placed on some of the narrow lines, or connected series of small elements forming lines, that have been introduced between wider and more important stripes of decoration. On the whole, nevertheless, there is at least a superficial appearance of a division into three longitudinal parts. It is therefore probable that though a conscious effort can not be postulated, the custom of using such divisions over a long period of time had become so ingrained a habit that at least an approach to such a procedure became more or less instinctive.

From above, downward the color keys and owners are: solid areas, red.

MRS. ALTA APPLEGATE, OWNER

Solid areas, red.

GEORGE A. H. FRASER, OWNER

Solid areas, red.

PEABODY MUSEUM OF HARVARD UNIVERSITY

Solid areas, red.

WILLIAM ROCKHILL NELSON GALLERY OF ART

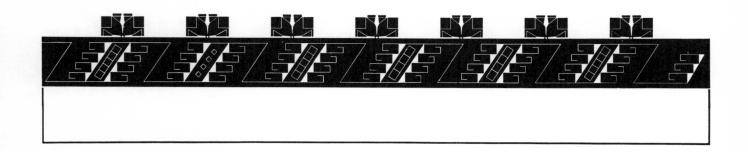

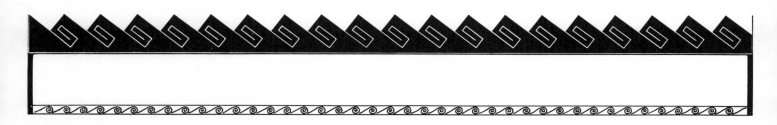

PLATE XXI

63

PLATE **XXII**

DESIGNS FROM WOOLEN MANTAS

The remarks accompanying the previous plate are equally applicable here. The first band figured is the only one of record in this class in which blocks of contrasting color have been incorporated.

The color keys and owners are indicated below, beginning at the top: solid areas, red; stippling, green.

N. B. STERN COLLECTION

Solid areas, red.

W. D. HOLLISTER COLLECTION

Solid areas, red.

FRED HARVEY COLLECTION

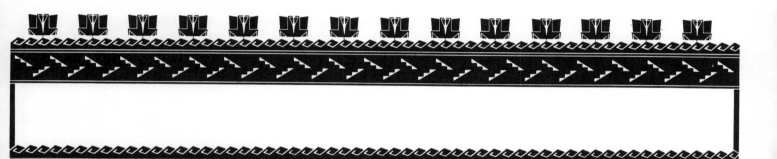

PLATE XXII

65

PLATE **XXIII**

DESIGNS FROM WOOLEN MANTAS

The three examples figured on this plate may all be classed as somewhat atypical in one regard or another. This is particularly true in respect to the one in the center. Although all the design-units and elements in this instance are good Indian design, there is not the slightest trace of zoning. Perhaps this particular specimen can be regarded as the exception that is said to prove the rule.

The remaining two, at the top and bottom, exhibit the usual zonal divisions but the composition and a number of features of design give a curiously different effect, setting them apart from any others studied. Not only is the design somewhat aberrant but some of the material used in embroidering is so seldom employed in this type of garment that these two examples are the only ones known in which this particular kind of yarn appears. In the band shown at the bottom of the plate a three-ply commercial yarn, in its day called Saxony, has been used throughout. The uppermost band, though largely worked in the usual handspun yarn has been pieced out at one end with some of that same three-ply material. Taking into consideration the originality of both designs and the mutual presence of Saxony yarn, it might be inferred that both were the work of a single individual. This particular kind of imported yarn was available to Indian weavers from about 1850 on until sometime around the middle of the 1870's, after which period its use was largely discontinued, as evidenced by its absence in most textiles that can be authentically dated as fabricated after that time.

Color keys are listed from above downward: solid areas, scarlet and vermillion; stippling, blue.

THE SOUTHWEST MUSEUM

Solid areas, red; stippling, blue.

MUSEUM OF THE AMERICAN INDIAN, HEYE FOUNDATION

Solid areas, vermillion; stippling, green.

THEODORE VAN SOELEN, OWNER

PLATE XXIII

PLATE XXIV

DESIGNS FROM WOOLEN MANTAS OF THE "REVIVAL" PERIOD

Following what was obviously the golden age of embroidery design on the woolen manta, a rapid decline set in, beginning about 1880, until in a few years the art itself became virtually extinct except for some work done on cotton fabrics.

In the early 1920's an attempt was made, with disappointing results, to revive Pueblo Indian embroidery with an especial emphasis with regard to work on wool. The failure of this revival may be attributed to at least two main factors; first, a lack of any economic return due to a loss of interest on the part of the Indians themselves because the embroidered wool manta had long since gone out of style, having been supplanted for many years by more easily obtained commercial garments such as gaily colored shawls or merely squares of printed fabrics; secondly, the new product was not particularly attractive either in design or coloring. This latter drawback may have been largely the result of a lack of knowledge of old design, a great majority of the examples exhibiting the finest tradition being by that time in the hands of museums or individuals where they were not available for reference and also because the material used for embroidering was confined to coarse four-ply commercial yarns with raw and garish coloring.

The three bands of decoration here shown are typical of the comparatively small number produced during the short period of the "revival." That at the bottom approaches most closely the ideals of the old classic style, including a division into three zones, but, on the other hand, the embroiderer has failed utterly to realize the origin and significance of the series of motifs that appear as the uppermost zone. The fact that the original of this motif was once a conventionalized floral adaptation appears to have been unrecognized. This is even more apparent in the two decorative bands above it.

Color key: solid areas, red; stippling, blue.

FRED K. HINCHMAN COLLECTION

The three-zoned design at the top of this plate clearly evinces a very distant acquaintance, if any, with the older and more elaborate types of decoration, or perhaps, through a lack of ambition or skill the embroiderer preferred such a simplified treatment as requiring less work.

Color key: solid areas, red; stippling, blue.

INDIAN ARTS FUND COLLECTION

Figured in the central position is another example from the "revival" period. It is quite evident that the maker must have been primed to outdo any competitor in the number of units of design used but the result is sadly lacking in dignity and not particularly pleasing. The three-zone formula has been entirely ignored and no resemblance to any floral concept is to be seen in the row of units at the top. The garment from which this was taken was exhibited at an "Indian Fair" in the early 1920's. Its present whereabouts is unknown.

Color key: solid areas, red; stippling, blue.

PLATE XXIV

69

PLATE XXV

DESIGNS FROM WOOLEN MANTAS, ZUÑI TYPE

Heretofore, all wool manta designs illustrated belong to what may be called the Acoma-Laguna school of decoration, one that can be traced as a logical development from a common basic system of traditional procedure. Those figured on this plate, on the contrary, do not appear on grounds of either structure or arrangement, to be definitely relatable to any particular decorative system.

The four examples appearing here, particularly the three upper, are typical of the Zuñian idea of what constitutes the best in decoration for woolen mantas. So restricted is the choice of decorative devices allowable to the craftsman in the village of Zuñi that all specimens examined have exhibited only combinations and regroupings of simple elemental units such as are shown here. There seems to be no valid reason why such a distinctly different type of design should have been adopted for the woolen article, when contemporary cotton mantas embroidered in this pueblo cannot be distinguished, because of their traditional style, from those of any other village where embroidery was practiced. Nor were the contacts between the Zuñi worker and areas, where the more decorative Acoma-Laguna type was being produced, so remote that that style could not have been easily taken over if desired. It is quite obvious that the less ornate was preferred.

Another distinctive difference may be seen in the consistent use of a single floral conventionalization instead of the doubled form characteristic of work from Acoma and Laguna. This is such a constant feature that it may usually serve as an identifying mark. It is quite probable that one or both of the bands shown on Plate XII (second and third from the bottom) were executed by Zuñi embroiderers.

Despite all divergencies from traditional structure, one thing deserves especial emphasis and that is the continued use of the traditional negative line pattern.

The corresponding color keys are given from above downward: solid areas, blue.

INDIAN ARTS FUND COLLECTION

Solid areas, blue.

LABORATORY OF ANTHROPOLOGY

Solid areas, blue.

INDIAN ARTS FUND COLLECTION

Solid areas, red.

FIELD MUSEUM OF NATURAL HISTORY

PLATE XXV

71

PLATE XXVI

DECORATIVE ACCESSORIES FROM WOOLEN MANTAS

All of the items shown on this plate can be considered as merely adjuncts to manta decoration. The designs shown in the several horizontally placed strips, six in number, were used parallel to the lateral borders of the garment to connect the upper and lower bands of embroidery. All make use of various European techniques. These six include every variation observed.

The two central figures were placed in the middle of the manta fabric, an idea possibly inspired by certain figures occurring on cotton mantas from Acoma. These latter, however, occupy a position, not in the center but nearer the upper band of embroidery. (See Plate VI.) European techniques were employed in both instances. The figure at the left was secured from an example in the American Museum of Natural History. The other occurs on the manta with the band of design, second from the bottom, on Plate XIX. Red was the sole color used for everything shown on this plate.

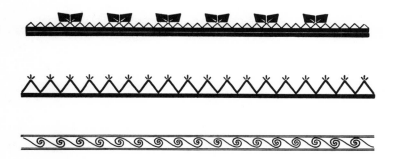

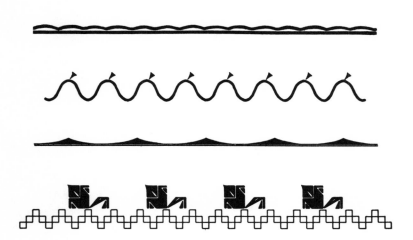

PLATE XXVI

73